LABOUR v. SINN FEIN

The Dublin General Strike 1913/14

The Lost Revolution

Terry McCarthy

Labour History Movement Pamphlet No.1

First edition published 1971

Second edition published 1975

This edition with amendments and additions published 2008

Copyright © Terry McCarthy 1971, 1975, 2008

Other publications about the Labour movement, including original pamphlet reprints and Trade Union emblems are available.

Cover Illustration: Will Dyson cartoon 1913

ISBN 978-0-9556923-0-7

Contents

Preface

I t's now some thirty-seven years since I wrote Labour v. Sinn Fein and Outcast Dublin. There have been some profound changes in the intervening years.

Then, the British TUC could boast a membership of 13 million, the left seemed on the ascendancy, we were still talking about the split in Sinn Fein Officials v Provisional, Ireland still sent her sons and daughters to seek employment in England by the thousand and Keynesian ideology was still the order of the day.

Since, the rise of monetarist philosophy and its implementation lead to major defeats for organised labour, the destruction of the manufacturing base and draconian anti-Trade Union legislation in line with the new ideology. There was also an unprecedented attack on all of the ideological, cultural, and political institutions of the left.

Now, Trade Union membership, in spite of a much larger workforce, runs at less than 7 million and despite having the fifth richest economy in the world workers in the UK enjoy worse conditions in terms of hours worked, age of retirement and disposable income in real terms than they did in the early seventies.

As always, there is hope.

As I write the Transport and General Workers' Union and Amicus have merged to form the general union Unite. For the first time in decades we have a giant general union that Tom Mann, James Connolly, Deliah Larkin and James Larkin would have been proud of. Who would have dreamed at the time when I began writing these pamphlets the success that Sinn Fein would have, and that the living standard for workers in Ireland would be above that of workers in the British mainland.

Friends and family (plus the brisk trade in my first edition on internet auction sites and the like) have encouraged me to rewrite and publish Labour v. Sinn Fein which I hope you enjoy. God knows what the next 30 years will bring!

Introduction

The Easter Rebellion in Dublin in 1916 is seen by many as the most crucial event in modern Irish history but the rebellion didn't happen in a political void, and the events prior to the First World War are key to understanding the development of nationalism at the expense of socialism, which prior to the outbreak of the First World War appeared to be the new dynamic force in politics.

The rebellion of 1916 confirmed events namely the removal of influence and power, in the institutional sense anyway, from the hands of the traditional home rule party into the hands of a more potent collection of nationalist groups which advocated a far more extreme approach to the relationship with Great Britain: such movements as Sinn Fein; the Gaelic League; the Gaelic Athletic Association and the Irish Republican Brotherhood. All of these groups went beyond simply the Home Rule policy of Redmond, the parliamentary successor of Parnell.

The rebellion, with other factors, such as the threat of conscription and the Catholic Church's attitude did much to change the grass roots opinion towards English rule, but it would be a false conclusion to accept as inevitable the move to Nationalism given the rise of the Socialist Labour Movement with its own paramilitary force, the Citizens' Army, under the leadership of Captain White, James Larkin, and finally, under the command of James Connolly.

Labour v. Sinn Fein

Sinn Fein was transformed during 1913 and 1914, the period of the labour unrest in Dublin, culminating in a six-month strike in which a third of the population was directly involved.

The Dublin Strike was not the biggest strike in terms of numbers in the period of industrial unrest before the First World War. What terrified employers, the State and some elements of the British Trades Union and Labour Movement was the fact that the strikers were linked to an armed force of workers, the Citizens' Army. This was alien to any preceding political or industrial dispute. It was the first time in Ireland's history that the main protagonists against the State were socialists and indeed armed ones.

The British intelligence service warned of the dangers of this strike, noting that this was not just an industrial dispute or rebellion but, if left its own devices, could lead to a Socialist revolution that might spread to the mainland.

Chapter 1
Labour and Capital

The development of manufacturing Capitalism in Ireland paralleled that of England. As in the United Kingdom, the Industrial Revolution threw up a new class: workers who realised the value and necessity of organisation.

In 1812, the Builders' and Plasterers' Guild made a report on their trade before and since the formations of the union - it urged that the English working classes should not be blamed for the misery brought about by English rule.

In 1824 Richard Smyth, Lord Mayor of Dublin, told a Select Committee: "the state of society among the working classes in Dublin is truly alarming". A Dublin solicitor named William Hall estimated that there were twenty-five or twenty-six distinctive unions with branches in the capital who had administered oaths and that "one trade union would take up the cause of another."(1) Owenite settlements were founded in Orbiston, Exeter, Ralahine, Assington, Cork and Dublin during the 1830's and the first Co-operative Society was founded in 1830 at Armagh. (2)

The imposed famines of the 1840's had decimated the population reducing it by 48%. It witnessed the demise of capital investment in industry. During the nineteenth century, more than three million Irish emigrated to America, and there are now more Irish in the United States than in Ireland.

The unparalleled destitution and sufferings of the Irish peasantry are an instructive example of the lengths to which the landlords and the liberal bourgeoisie of a "ruling" nation will go. (3) The English ruling class now designated Ireland to become an agrarian adjunct to its own financial development. England was to become the 'workshop of the world' and all other countries were to become for England what Ireland already was: a market for her manufactured goods, supplying her in return with raw materials and food. "England, the great manufacturing centre of an agricultural world, with an ever-increasing number of corn and cotton growing states revolving around her, the industrial sun. What a glorious prospect!" noted Frederick Engel's. Despite this grave setback organised Irish labour developed in theory and practice.

By 1863 the Dublin United Trades Association had been formed and in 1868 joined the British Trade Union Congress. Belfast did not develop its Trade Union Council until 1881. By the end of the 1880's most Irish towns had their own Trade Union Councils (5) and by 1895 the Irish Trade Unionists were strong enough to form the Irish Trade Union Congress. It is estimated that at the time there were 93 unions in Ireland with a total membership of 17,476. In 1900 the British TUC invited the Irish TUC to re-corporate itself, an invitation which was refused.

Ireland remained endlessly troublesome to the British establishment, though after 1890 the explosive unrest of the years of the Land League and Parnell seemed to have been defused by Irish political quarrels and by a powerful combination of repression and far-reaching agrarian reform.

Labour and Capital

The violent quasi-general strikes in Belfast 1907, the transport strike in Liverpool in 1911 and the other major industrial disputes of the period shook the establishment but in no way did they sense revolution on the horizon, even though the victory of the Miners' general strike in 1912 made Prime Minister Asquith physically weep. In fact the greatest threat against the Crown came from those who considered themselves the most loyal, with the armed refusal of Ulster Protestants and their allies in the military to accept parliamentary decisions which threatened their privileged position. (6 & 7)

Unfortunately the establishment within the English Trade Union movement accepted the imperial view of Empire and its relationship with Ireland as laid down by the State, only differing from it in the way its poverty should be relieved, offering only liberal reform based on paternalism. Karl Marx took a totally different view. He thought it was in the class interests of the English working class to dissolve the link with Ireland and indeed the union itself: "I have become more and more convinced the English working class can never do anything decisive until it separates its policy with regard to Ireland and takes the initiative in dissolving the union established in 1801. This must be done, not as a matter of sympathy with Ireland, but as a demand made in the interests of the English proletariat. And Ireland freedom is a prerequisite for English working class freedom".(8)

The English New Union Movement of the 1880's appeared to have freed itself from the conservative elements of the skilled unions who had worn the epitaph 'the respectable working class' with pride (Frederick Engel's made the poignant observation that "the current trade union leaders would rather be inside the mansion house at a Lord Mayor's banquet then outside demonstrating against it").(8)

11

The new union movement had a much broader base for organisation, and with education and the right leadership it could change the ideology from liberalism to socialism.

A major component of new unionism came from Irish émigrés and their descendants, especially in south-east and east London. The gas, dock, and match industries enjoyed a very high percentage of Irish and Anglo-Irish workers. The Stevedores Union formed in London in 1872 was an offshoot of the Irish Land and League movement and was almost exclusively Catholic (9) and there were also small Catholic Skilled Workers Labour Associations around shipbuilding and repair in south-east and east London: these workers originally emigrated from Cork (for various reasons, labour and social historians have concentrated on the Whitechapel community and its important role in the development of socialist theory and practice, unfortunately this has often been done at the expense of other ethnic groups in south-east and east London).

The 1889 Dock Strike would not have succeed without the financial assistance of the Australian Trade and Labour Movement where the Irish dimension was crucial, their contributions equalled millions of pounds in today's currency.(10)

The same could be said of the Liverpool New Union Movement. Tom Mann had agitated for one giant union before, during, and after the dock strike of 1889 which did not please the individual General Secretaries. His Minority Movement of rank and file trade unionists pleased them even less. The term Syndicalist is often used when describing Tom Mann prior to his membership of the Communist Party, theory not being strength of the British Labour Movement, and this description was typical of the shorthand used. The nuances in theory of de Leon and Soral did not enjoy a great following amongst the Labour Movement hierarchy.

Another paradox in the development of the New Union Movement was the role of the Catholic Church. Under the auspices of Cardinal Manning, the Church in England took a more conciliatory stand on the development and role of trade unions and indeed Manning was supportive of Joseph Arch in the development of the Agricultural Workers Union (11). Manning was also supportive in the unionisation of unskilled labour in east and south-east London, especially amongst dock workers. Given the large number of Catholics in these areas the support of the Catholic Church cannot be underestimated notably in the formation of the Dockers Union and the winning of the 1889 Dock Strike.

During the many New Union Movement disputes the encyclical of Pope Leo XIII was often quoted (see appendix). This applied to the match workers in their dispute in 1888, the majority of which were girls and women who were Irish or of Irish descent. In fact, the area was described as a fenian barracks (12). By the time of the Dublin strike this infallible papal statement was interpreted to suit Capitalism (12&13).

Chapter 2
Labour v. Labour

T he radicalism of the New Union Movement had been short lived. Ben Tillett and the other former leaders of the New Union Movement, with the exception of Tom Mann, Tom McCarthy and John Burns, moved inexorably to the right, best demonstrated by their attitude toward the Dublin Strike and the First World War which was to split the British Labour Movement.

The Pro-War Committee, made up of Trade Union and Labour leaders, endorsed the First World War calling for volunteers and denouncing strike action as unpatriotic. (1)

John Burns resigned his parliamentary seat over the issue of the First World War whereas his former comrades were scrabbling to obtain seats in parliament - the irony being many of their members, men and women, had not yet attained the vote.

In 1912 George Lansbury had resigned his parliamentary seat over the issue of adult suffrage (women and poor working men) and suffered defeat in the subsequent by-election. Lansbury was a keen supporter of Larkin and defended him and the strike through his recently founded newspaper, the Daily Herald. He was totally opposed to involvement in the First World War and along with (2) Keir Hardie openly criticised the pro-war group of trade union leaders and Labour parliamentarians. Hardie went even further calling for a general strike against the war and frequently visited Dublin during the strike supporting Larkin and the Dublin strikers.(3)

The new old guard all became parliamentarians. Harry Gosling was third time lucky when he was elected in Wapping with the support of the Catholic Church (to get an idea of Gosling's patronising view of organised Irish labour and the Irish themselves, read his autobiography, especially the chapter General Council). Gosling becoming Transport Minister in the first Labour government, and they all moved progressively to the right.(4) To ensure their dominance a small group of right-wingers, the majority being former New Union Movement leaders, created a small group within the TUC named the Parliamentary Committee. Gosling, a prominent member, describes it in the following manner "The Parliamentary Committee always aimed at making itself the national organ for the development of British industrial trade unionism, and was generally looked upon as the "Front Bench" or the informal Cabinet of the Trade Union Congress. " (1)

Ben Tillet moved in even murkier waters; he enjoyed a close association with Horatio Bottomley, a corrupt businessman and newspaper proprietor and the prospective Liberal candidate for South Hackney. Bottomley appointed Tillett to edit the 1903 May Day edition of his newspaper, the Sun. Later that year Tillett spoke at an election rally in support of Bottomley and was a named Bottomley supporter.

Tillett's actions did not go down well with the Labour Representation Committee (L.R.C) of which Tillett was supposedly a member. The L.R.C, who were contesting the seat, and Charles Home, secretary of the Hackney Trades Council, sent a private letter to Tillett outlining their concerns about Bottomley and his dubious business dealings. Tillett immediately showed this to Bottomley who then

15

threatened to sue. Home called his bluff and Bottomley withdrew his threat.(5)

Bottomley and Tillett were so close that Bottomley invited Tillett's daughter Jenny to live in his large house: unfortunately for Ben Jenny was her own woman and was very close to Tom Mann (another reason why Tillett had such distain for Mann, his politics and friends). Jenny told Mann of the meetings that went on in Bottomley's home, especially of one group of guests which included Hyndman the Marxist Businessman, Havelock Wilson of the seamen's union, Perkins, Houston and Cox (Bottomley's minders and fixers) and a certain Maundy Gregory who was a founder member of the British Intelligence Service.(6)

Victor Grayson also made infrequent visits. Grayson however fell out with the pro-war section when he went absent at a large open-air meeting in support of the war. Maundy Gregory was the prime mover in the blackmailing of Grayson over his homosexuality. Much can be said for the integrity of Larkin that despite all the gossip and innuendo Larkin willingly shared a platform with Grayson in 1914 where he spoke of Grayson's achievements (7) and was one of the few trusted former comrades who knew the whereabouts of Grayson in the years after the First World War.

Ben Tillett was proud to declare himself a Christian Socialist and was quick to denounce others for their loose living: these included Tom Mann and Victor Grayson, neither of which ever publicly condemned Tillett for his own adulterous lifestyle as although Ben Tillett lived with his wife and mother of his nine children, he was also having an affair with Australian opera singer Eva Newton who bore him four children, and after breaking up with Eva, Tillett took a second mistress.

Chapter 3
Sinn Fein and the Church

The Irish Left was frustrated and angered that nationalist leaders did not distinguish between the oppressing Imperialist State and the working-class of that State which was equally exploited, and that they would willingly played the race and religious card to gain popularity. Arthur Griffiths and Patrick Pearse were masters of this tactic as was Edward Carson, leader of the Ulster loyalists.

Sinn Fein was founded by Arthur Griffith in 1905 with the object of 'the re-establishment of the independence of Ireland',(1) under a fifteen point programme which was:

1.   A protective system for Irish industries and commerce enforced by the powers held by local authorities, harbour boards, and other bodies;

2.   An Irish consular service;

3.   A mercantile marine;

4.   The general survey of Ireland and development of its mineral resources;

5.   A national bank and stock exchange;

6.   A national civil service, to be instituted by national qualifying and local competitive examination, under the local authorities;

7.   National courts of arbitration;

8.   A National system of insurance;

9.   National control of transit;

10.   Development of fisheries;

11.   Reform on national lines of education;

12.   Non-consumption of objects paying duty to the British Exchequer;

13.   Stoppage of enlistment;

14.   Non-recognition of the British Parliament and the establishment of a National Assembly;

15.   Abolition of the poorhouse system and employment of the able-bodied in reclamation work, afforestation, etc.

Griffith advocated a dual monarchy system for Ireland.(2) He urged the adoption of a Hungarian policy, proposing the tactic of abstention from the Parliament. These aims were far less extreme than those put forward during and after the First World War.

Sinn Fein was made up in its early days mainly of journalists and the young intelligencia from the middle classes and it was still very much a minority movement commenting on events which for the present were out of its control. The kernel of Sinn Fein's ideology was that the nation is predominant, demonstrated in the seven points put forward in the September 13th Edition of 'Sinn Fein' which were:

1.   That the true interests of Capital and Labour are not inimical but interdependent;

2.   That neither Capital nor Labour has fully realised the fact, and that the realisation must be forced upon them by the Nation;

3.   That in any pitched battle between Capital and Labour, with no intervening force, Capital must always win;

4.   That the nation cannot afford that anyone of its sections should be enslaved by the other, and therefore cannot permit such a pitched battle;

5.   That the right of Labour to a fair share of the joint product of Labour and Capital is clear and inalienable, and it is the duty of the Nation (or the State) to see that it gets it;

6.   That the Strike as a weapon of offence is useless and as a weapon of defence is only the last resort;

7.   That the path of progress for labour is not along the line of destruction (the strike), since it cannot destroy without, like Samson, burying itself in the ruins, but along the line of construction (co-operation), by which it can bring its own strength gradually nearer to the level of the strength of Capital. (3)

With this change in ideology came a political awareness of the uses to which labour could be put to help Sinn Fein. The Labour Movement which had been so successful at winning over the hearts and minds of the mass of the working population of Dublin was daily losing heart. True, they gave Larkin all the support and indeed more than could be asked but industrial action in terms of sympathetic strikes from the English trade union movement were not widely forthcoming. The best that the English trade union movement could do was to offer food.

That is not to say there was no dissent inside Sinn Fein. The left-wing of Sinn Fein led by Eamonn Ceannt wrote attacking Griffith and supporting the working classes. Griffith continued to debate with

Ceannt through Sinn Fein (the paper) during the early periods of the strike,(4) but as the strike entered into its gloomy phase before the recognition of defeat had become public Sinn Fein began to attack socialism and the labour movement. "I deny that Socialism is a remedy for the existent evils or any remedy at all. I deny that Capital and Labour are in their nature antagonistic" and "In the year 1913 we are in Ireland back almost in the economic position that we occupied in 1725, when with a population of two and a half million people we were forced to import food to feed ourselves."(5) Sinn Fein denounced both trade unions and socialism as English and therefore institutions and doctrines that were anti-Irish both morally and culturally.

To accuse the Roman Catholic Church of sheer indifference and inhumanity would be absurd, given the good works undertaken in Dublin. Nuns would often bring the slum-dweller into the world, nurse him when he was sick and lay him out when he died, then comfort his widow. All these things were done with love and genuine affection. Their loyalty was blind as was their analysis of the political situation which caused so much misery.

An accusation of corruption because of shares owned by certain clergy in individual firms affected by the Labour dispute would also be misrepresentative of the truth. There may have been one or two cases where vested interests gave sway over honest interpretation of faith but this was not the root cause of the Church's attitude.

We must look at the ideology of the Church and then analyse its behaviour. The Church believed in first and foremost in saving souls, and it was spiritual salvation more than social change which concerned it most. The encyclical of Leo XIII which caused much debate during the labour dispute: the Labour Movement interpreting it as a justification for the trade union movement and socialism, using quotes from the encyclical such as "Justice, therefore demands that the interests of the poorer classes should be carefully watched over by the administration, so that they who contribute so largely to the advantage of the community may themselves share in the benefits which they create that, being housed, clothed, and enabled to sustain life, they may find their existence less hard and more endurable."(6).. This would be countered by the Irish Church, who pointed to Pope Leo XIII, who had said that "the idea so prevalent that class was naturally hostile to class, and that the wealthy and the working-man are intended by Nature to live in mutual conflict was a great mistake. The direct contrary was the truth "(7), and to call the encyclical a supportive document for socialism would indeed be wrong as a following quote from the encyclical shows clearly: (8)"It is clear that the main tenet of Socialism, community of goods, must be utterly rejected, since it only injures those whom it would seem to benefit, is directly contrary to the natural rights of mankind, and would introduce confusion and disorder into the commonweal...It would throw open the door to envy, to mutual invective, and to discord: the sources of wealth themselves would run dry, for no one would have any interest in exerting his talents or his industry and that ideal equality about which they entertain pleasant dreams would be in reality the levelling down of all to a like condition of misery and degradation."(9)

The Church was consistent in its attacks on the labour movement especially in the period of the strike when it gave priority to attack on its leader James Larkin, (10) who to them was almost the devil's advocate. He was married to a protestant by civil ceremony,(11) an admitted Socialist, he was to them by implication an atheist, by insinuation an advocate of free love and by innuendo an abortionist. He was the enemy of God, man and the nation.(12) Dr. Clancy, the bishop of Sligo, denounced Larkin as a socialist and forbade attendance of the union meetings. Larkin himself always claimed to be a good Catholic, and his personal life was exemplary - a t-totaller, he had made himself unpopular amongst the workers by banning prostitutes from ships when in port. He saw no conflict between the religion of the Catholic Church and Marxism. "I stand by the cross and the Marx. I belong to the Catholic Church."(13) But this fell on deaf ears as far as the Church was concerned.(14)

Connolly on the other hand occupied a more ambiguous position on religion. He regarded Catholicism as simply a natural cultural phenomenon. (15) Nevertheless, he declared himself a Catholic though a dogmatic Marxist (influenced greatly by De Leon, when in America,) the leader of the Marxist Irish Socialist Party. He had curiously enough a liaison both with the Church and Sinn Fein, yet this is not so strange when one looks at some of Connolly's statements at the time: "the term Protestant is almost a convertible term with Toryism, lick-spittle loyalty, servile worship of aristocracy and hatred of all that savours of genuine political independence on the part of the 'lower classes'", while, "Catholicism…is almost synonymous with rebellious tendencies, zeal for democracy, and intense feeling of solidarity, with all strivings upward of those who toil".

Almost forgotten is the important role of Peter Larkin who was the mainstay of the work in Belfast undertaken by the Irish Transport Workers Union and it was of course Jim Larkin who managed to unite both Catholic and Protestant workers and lay the foundations for a united trade union movement, though short-lived. "Thousands of Protestant workers, instead of swelling the throngs of the "glorious twelfth", paraded with their Catholic fellow-workers in protest against their bosses." But this tended to alienate the Church and Sinn Fein, if anything, even more.

It is in this light that the Church must be judged, not in its personal handling of the situation but its blind ideology, which obeyed without question, ignoring the facts that surrounded it daily. The irony was that the Church knew more than anybody about the terrible social conditions and misery that prevailed in Dublin. (16)

Note: There has never been a work done on either Peter or Deliah Larkin, who have tended to slip into insignificance, mainly, I feel, because of their attitude to the Easter Rising and their open hostility to Connolly's links with the Sinn Fein and I.R.B.

Chapter 4
Right v. Left
Sexton and Larkin

I have personalised Sexton and Larkin as they fully represented the two distinct sections of the trade and labour movement during the period.

The development of Dockers Unions' in Liverpool paralleled that in London, small unions being formed as early as the 1840's and 1850's, separate elitist stevedores, none of which developed, most disappearing without trace.(1)

The New Union Movement of the late 1880's gave new life to organising dockers and general workers labourers into unions. The formation of the National Union of Dock Labourers in 1889 was an important turning point. Like its counterpart in London, it was predominantly Catholic, with a high percentage being of Irish descent. The union leadership shared the sectarian views of those in London in relation to merging with other unions coming out of the New Union Movement, despite the pleas of Tom Mann and Tom McCarthy for one giant union.

James Sexton had a small coal business (his parents were small business people) at the time of the unions formation.(2) Sexton, like so many others, became a member as he was a casual at the docks when business was bad. Shortly after, Sexton's business went bankrupt and he then dedicated all of his time and talents into the union and in 1893 he was appointed general-secretary to the union.(3)

By 1913 Sexton judged the world as it was when he first began organising and campaigning. For him, the world was a much better place; after all, they now had their own party with Members of Parliament of which he was soon to be one, and before too long all working men, and indeed women, would have the vote, what in the past had been a dream, a Labour government, was now a distinct possibility and once parliamentary power had been achieved society could be changed totally and the worst aspects of capitalism would be abolished.

The trade union movement was now bigger, richer and more powerful than it had ever been. Trade union membership affiliated to the TUC was 2,232000 members from 207 Unions. The setbacks of Taff Vale and the Osborne judgment had been overcome.(4)

Sexton's section of the movement argued this was not the time for mass strikes, especially those accompanied by any form of civil disobedience. Interestingly, Sexton states in his autobiography that by the 1880's, having "realised the utter hopelessness of the Irish physical force movement I joined constitutional movement heart and soul".

Sexton's father was a supporter of the Fenian movement in Liverpool and a devout Catholic; his son inherited both these traits. When Sexton's camp were in ascendance and they controlled the TUC and most of the industrial unions, though not all, they began to influence their authority outside the industrial sector. They insisted that the trade union college at Oxford Ruskin College did not teach revolutionary ideas, for future leadership after all was to be in their image; this caused a strike by the students and members of the faculty in 1909. The strike was unsuccessful; however it led to the formation of the Labour Colleges movement, the Plebs League. Decades later this Socialist Educational facility was in turn destroyed by the TUC (4) (I suggested to J P Miller he must have been devastated by this, he turned with a wry smile on his face: "young man," he said, "you can always tell if you're doing the right thing because those bastards will always try to wreck it").

The jingoism shown in the First World War by Sexton, Tillett, Wilson and Co, their violent hostility to those opposed to it, even towards pacifists and religious objectors, demonstrated their new conservatism, gradualism was now the order of the day, they viewed those who put forward a Socialist Programme as the enemies within, hotheads, followers of foreign ideologies, who would through their agitation destroy all the gains that they had made through the reformist parliamentary road and they thought they should be to be dealt with accordingly.

The TUC Leadership had reverted back to the days of Robert Applegarth, aptly named the junta, and the politics of the new model unions of the 1860's and 1870's - the paradox being that they now displayed the same attitudes and prejudices displayed and used against them when they helped launch the New Union Movement.

By his late-twenties James Larkin was doing fairly well given the standards of the time. He was committed family man, a foreman in the docks where he was known to be a diligent worker. But Larkin wasn't happy with society, no matter what his material situation might have been. Larkin was lucky; he had a family of socialists around him, especially his sister Deliah. He was juxtaposed to the idea that society was getting better for him and there was poverty everywhere, (5) especially in all the major cities in the United Kingdom, and for the life of him he couldn't see where the reforms were in Dublin and the rest of Ireland.

In 1905 Larkin's life changed: "'Jim' Larkin crashed upon the British public with the devastating force and roar of a volcano exploding without even a preliminary wisp of smoke. He swept down upon us, indeed, with the startling suddenness of the eruption of Mont Pelee, and, proportionally, his activities were hardly less serious in their results" was James Sexton's back handed compliment to Larkin in his autobiography.

During this period the employers in the Liverpool docks launched a counter-attack against Unionism and union recognition. Larkin's employer embarked upon this policy allowing non-union Labour to work in the dock and the dock workers took unofficial strike action.

Sexton arrived on the scene and sought to achieve victory by citing health and safety and union recognition agreements, which were ignored by the employer. Larkin supported the strike and began organising the foremen and although this was not a major strike Larkin's name and reputation as an agitator and organiser spread throughout Liverpool; the die was now cast.

Larkin was offered a job as organiser for Sexton's National Union of Dock Labourers which paid a pound a week less than he was already earning. Sexton had other important assignments for Larkin besides recruiting members and looking after the membership; Larkin was his campaign manager for his successful entry into local politics.

27

Sexton was one of the first two Labour councillors elected onto Liverpool city council and was only narrowly defeated in his bid to become Liverpool MP. Sexton was glowing in his compliments to Larkin, stating openly that he would not have achieved the success he had done without Jim's organisational and oratory skills (Larkin was a great asset in Victor Grayson's successful campaign to win the Cone Valley parliamentary seat 1907).(6)

To Larkin, Sexton at best was foolish at worst corrupt. Larkin after a short while working with Sexton concluded he (Sexton) didn't and wouldn't understand or represent the true demands of his members, and what ever his history was, he was now an impediment to action, recruitment and real change.

Larkin was fortunate when he teamed up with Marxist Socialist James Connolly. Previous to the close working relationship with Connolly, Larkin had shown little interest in Socialist ideology although he had been a declared Socialist from the age of seventeen and a member of the Independent Labour Party. Connolly soon changed that; their partnership culminating in the harmony of theory and practice.

Larkin's friendship with Tom Mann and members of the I.W.W did not enhance his reputation to the TUC leadership, Lenin's support went unnoticed; after all he was just another Russian refugee living in East London. Their concerns were more the fact that the French and other European Syndicalists and Anarcho-Syndicalists supported him. (7)

It was obvious that two such different ideologies, that of the TUC and Sexton, and that of Larkin now that he was teamed up with James Connolly, could not co-exist. Larkin was to find out just how vicious the 'new old-guard' could be.

28

Larkin's organisational skills were demonstrated at Preston in 1906 when he opened up a branch of 900 Dockers, achieving recognition and then a closed shop. At this stage there was nothing but praise for Larkin, who was equally successful in Scotland. Larkin was then that sent to Ireland; it was Sexton's plan to launch a major recruitment drive and at first all went to plan as Larkin was a great success in Dublin, Cork and Belfast where the men soon took to him . It was in Dublin that the rift between the Sexton camps view of the role of trade unions and that of Larkin, Connolly and Tom Mann's began.

There was great industrial unrest in Belfast during 1907 and it is true that Larkin fuelled the flames; it was not just Dockers and transport workers in dispute, most of it unofficial club, the Royal Irish Constabulary mutinied and there was much violence and civil disobedience. The board of trade was brought in to conciliate. Sexton complained that the dispute would ruin the N.U.D.L as the costs incurred were over £7,000, although contributions from sections of the labour movement plus a levy on the members involved brought this sum down considerably.

Sexton was now in charge; he deliberately misinformed sections of the strikers that he had negotiated an honourable settlement when he had not done so. Larkin was furious; he publicly made his views known and Sexton experienced a very uncomfortable union annual conference, where he stated: "As the high priest of the institution I have been that target for every delegate with a bee in his bonnet"(8). Despite Sexton's misgivings, union membership grew.

Larkin was now dispatched to Dublin where he was in charge of a branch of 2,700 members however when a strike and lock-out took place, Sexton intervened as the employers had stated that they wouldn't talk directly to Larkin and Sexton complied with their wishes stating that; "wise counsel would prevail to save us from the reputation of the Belfast Dockers dispute."

By now, Larkin's card was marked, though he was still having successes as with the establishment of a branch in Cork with 800 members with a partially successful strike. Larkin now put his energy into helping the Dublin Carters who were in dispute; Sexton made it plain he did once he did not want another Belfast. Tom Mann stated: "Sexton always wanted to wait another season before he had to fight." Larkin was informed he was expected to consult Sexton and the executive of where and when he was to address workers meetings. Larkin's request for strike money for Cork members was rejected; Sexton cited the reason being that he was not consulted beforehand, a claim which Larkin challenged. Larkin was instructed to leave Ireland for Scotland; Larkin refused, stating that he was too busy recruiting, organising and leading unskilled labour in Dublin. He talked openly of an Irish Federation of Labour - one big union.

In December 1908 Larkin was suspended from the union and immediately formed the Irish Transport and General Workers' Union. The members voted with their feet; Sexton's union was confined to the much smaller ports. Sexton and his supporters would not however give up without a fight.

Larkin was arrested and charged with conspiracy and fraud in 1909. The Crown's case was the Dockers in Cork had paid £170 as subscriptions to the Cork branch of the N U D L which the Crown asserted had not legally existed. Sexton, who was subpoenaed, stated that Larkin had not informed him or the executive of the existence of such a branch, nor had he sent the money to Liverpool as according to the union's rules. Larkin was given 12 months hard labour, later reduced to three months.

Sexton was not yet finished. He sued Frank Pearce and the Northern Publishing Company for libel in relation to a pamphlet titled 'James Larkin, a Labour leader and an honest man', which alleged Sexton had engineered the prosecution against Larkin. Pearce lost the case and was ordered to pay £200 damages.(9)

Sexton was instrumental in developing Catholic action in the UK which was fervently anti-socialist and anti-communist, and spent much of his life developing this semi-secret society; perhaps its greatest triumph was financing and organising the successful campaign to wrest control from the Communists from the electricians union and power stations.(10)

Given this, the outcome of the TUC inquiry into the Dublin Strike was determined before it began.

Chapter 5
Dublin 1913

D ublin, capital city of England's oldest and most exploited colony physically and culturally, rows of decaying Georgian terraces, once monuments to Dublin's prosperity, and now shamefaced witnesses to Dublin's absolute decay. The buildings themselves seemed to be trying to hide Dublin's secret, hiding as they did row upon row of rotten slums. Architectural delights of another day had become dirty, decayed, wretched tenements - old, rotten, permeated with physical and moral corruption.

The poor crowded in these foul dwellings in incredible numbers for Dublin's housing was worse than that of Glasgow, London or Liverpool; and from this background arose the greatest industrial dispute in Irish History.

Dublin's population of 304,802 (1) could not have been more divided geographically as well as socially if it had been planned. The city was divided into two halves by the Liffee. In the south side of the city the respectable middle ¬and some skilled working-class lived in grand Georgian houses with beautiful Italian-designed plaster relief's. In the north side the plaster relief's were now somewhat faded and the overcrowded houses now bore the name tenements. The tenements housed the unskilled, the casual and the very poor.

Dublin 1913

The working population was reckoned to be 194,250 - 63% of the total population (2) which was broken down in the following way:

Skilled Workers	30%
Unskilled Workers	30%
Casual Workers	25%
Very Poor	15%

One third, or about 101,000, lived in single room accommodation and over 30,000 people out of the total population were evicted each year.(3) Dublin was a trading rather than an industrial city, the bulk of the labour force was employed in the carrying, or transporting, trade. Only 9,397 men were employed in industry - printing, engineering, clothing, furnishing, and leather tanning. (2)

Unemployment was exceptionally high in Dublin; up to 20%. (1) The reason for this was Dublin was more a commercial, distributing and shipping centre rather than a manufacturing city. Except in brewing and biscuit-making, its productive power was comparatively low and most of its factories were small and gave little manual employment. Unlike cities in Great Britain and even in Ulster its wage-earning population was over-whelming male with no more than occasional openings for women and young female workers.

The means test took no account of the size of the family so a labourer with a family of six children with an average income of 25 shillings per week would be in a worse position than a labourer with no children earning 20 shillings per week. The purchasing power of the pound had fallen by 3s, 9d since 1906 and food prices went up by 25% between 1905-1912.(8) General labourers, the great bulk of the wage-earners, were rarely paid more than 20 shillings a week and they averaged between 15 to 18 shillings a week.

Because of the scarcity of employment for women thousands of families had to exist on no more than 15 shillings a week and cases were recorded of total family earnings as low as ten shillings and less. Actual cases noted in the sparse official reports of the time show: 'a van driver, with mother-in-law and three children, in constant employment at 15 shillings a week, paying 2/6 rent, and having tea, bread and butter for breakfast, with cheap American bacon and cabbage or occasionally herrings for dinner, and tea and bread for evening meal or supper';(4)'a coal porter with wife and four children, irregularly employed at 18 shillings a week, paying 2/6d rent, with bread, butter and tea for breakfast, bacon and cabbage, and sometimes fish, for dinner, and bread, butter and tea for 3rd and last meal for the day'; 'a labourer with wife and four children, in constant work in summer and irregular work in winter, at 16 shillings a week, paying 136d rent, having tea and bread and occasionally butter, for breakfast, fish for dinner and meat on Sundays, with oatmeal porridge and buttermilk for supper'. (1)

Ironically, Irish bacon was beyond the price of most workers. Their bacon was low grade American at 5d or 6d a lb. With their tea, they took condensed skimmed milk with little or no fats. Mothers were advised by doctors not to give this to infants, but as lack of women's employment kept most, of them in their one-room homes, the majority of infants were breast-fed and mortality among these was relatively low within the labouring category.

Finding figures for what were classified as the very poor is impossible and the figures for the casual workers must be treated as very much a general average. Many people I interviewed, kindly introduced to me by the I.T.W Union, spoke of diets of potatoes and cocoa and in fact the strike brought to them in terms of relief luxuries such as meat and boots that they'd never experienced before. Of course, this was amongst the poorest section of the community and there was very much real hardship and suffering experienced by the majority of workers especially the respectable working class whose suffering was increased by their humiliation at accepting charity and being categorised with the very poor of the Dublin tenements. (5)

Labourers and their families could rarely afford to eat meat. The total cost of rents, food and coal averaged as 93% of the average in London, yet the average skilled man in Dublin earned only 79% of London tradesman's wage, and Dublin labourers only 66% of the London labourers' wage. These figures, from the Report of the Board of Trade Ed. 6955, prompted the conclusion: '...These figures go to show that Dublin labourers do not live in one room because they choose to do so, but because as a rule no choice is open to them'.(5)

The returns of the 1911 Census (Vo VIII) give the proportion of the population living as such as:

in London 13.4%;
in Edinburgh 21.9;%
in Dublin 33.9%.

In the Report of the Public Health Department of the Dublin Corporation for 1911, we find that::

12,296 persons were living 4 in one room;
11,335 persons were living 5 in one room;
8,928 persons were living 6 in one room;

5,978 persons were living 7 in one room;

3,448 persons were living 8 in one room;

1,314 persons were living 9 in one room;

450 persons were living 10 in one room;

176 persons were living 11 in one room;

60 persons were living 12 in one room.

The report noted: 'About 44,000 souls altogether living in this intensely over crowded state. The very high proportion of deaths per 1,000 under five years belonging to this class is therefore not surprising one'.

As well as enjoying the onerous title of Europe's worst-housed populous Dublin had an equal claim to ill-fame with its figures for health and death.

By 1911 Dublin's death-rate had risen to 27.6 per 1,000 when Calcutta's, infested with plague and cholera, was 27 and in Europe the next highest to Dublin's was 26.3 in Moscow. Of the deaths in Dublin 41.9% occurred in pauper workhouses, lunatic asylums and other institutions for 'the diseased in body and mind', as against 22% in similar conditions in England. (6) Every year about 2,600 babies under the age of five died in Dublin, 9 out of every 10 of them belonging to the working classes. In proportion to the population, for every baby that died in an upper-class home and for every three babies that died in middle-class homes no less than fourteen died in the homes of labourers. That was the case for children up to 5 years. However, out of every four children born only three ever reached the age of five. Of the babies less than a year old, for every 1000 births there were 140 or more deaths of babies under one year. In 1909, the figure was 141 per 1,000 in Dublin, as compared with 139 in Belfast, 126 in Cork, 122 in Edinburgh (in 1908) and 108 in London.

In a report to the Public Health Committee, for the period ending 16th August 1913: 'the death rate from certain infections or epidemic diseases – nearly all in the case of children'. The Irish Independent carried the story:

"In a season of exceptional warmth, there was usually in Dublin a high death rate from diarrhoeal diseases, especially among infants. There were in the fortnight ended last Saturday, 47 deaths from these diseases. The early decomposition of food owing to the heat must account for a good deal of the mischief, but Sir Charles Cameron (head of the Public Health Committee) once more calls attention to the baneful activity of the house-fly as a disease carrier. It was stated at a meeting of the Dublin Committee for the Prevention of Infantile Mortality the other night that on an average 660 of the 11,000 babies born in Dublin every year dies within twelve months of birth. No small proportion of this wastage of child life occurs during the occasional hot spells of our fickle summers. In the case of congenitally weak children, the mortality may not be preventable, but there is no doubt about it that care of the milk with which children are fed would save many lives. Ignorance on the part of mothers gives the greatest trouble to the voluntary health visitors of the Dublin Committee for the Prevention of Infant Mortality. The good ladies who perform the work of mercy of visiting poor mothers must often find that the instruction they impart as to the care of infants is as necessary as the relief they can give to the destitute. It is not out of place, in any case, that Sir Charles Cameron should repeat once more his warning of how dangerous the house-fly can be to life, and especially to child life, by infecting food".

While in no way dismissing the dangers of the house-fly or the affects of exceptional warm weather one can hardly say that the head of the Public Health Committee was in any way tackling the basic problems that lay behind Dublin's appalling health record - its slums, under-nourished children, lack of welfare facilities and sanitary conditions generally, both at home and at school.

The Church, once again is silent over this issue, although the principle welfare organisation and being familiar with the fundamental problem of Dublin's poorer citizens does not speak out on their behalf with its obvious authority.

The attitude of respectable Dublin is amply demonstrated by the way it deals with certain offences. Bearing in mind the references made by Sir Charles Cameron about the care of milk 'Mr. Burke, Assistant Law Adviser to the Corporation, called attention at the Southern Police Court to the case of Mary A. Farrell, of Francis Street, fined £100 on a charge of milk adulteration, March 5th last. It would be remembered, he said, that the fine would be reduced to £10 if the defendant agreed to get out of the business. He understood that the condition had been complied with, the defendant having sold her cows, farm and dairy. Mr. E.H. Burne, for the defendant, asked his worship to forego the fine, having regard to what happened. Mr. Drury said this woman had employed these people to adulterate the milk which she was selling, and was making a profit of fifty per cent thereby. A fine of £5.00 by consent was imposed'. (7)

Then there was the case when 'Haim Sereno, manager of the Queen's Park Picturedrome, was summoned on Tuesday before the Manchester city magistrates for contravening one of the conditions of his license, granted under the cinematograph Act. The specific allegation was that he allowed eight children under the age of 14 to attend the "second" performance at the theatre on the night of July 12th without being accompanied by a parent or guardian. Inspector Dorricott proved the case. The defendant was fined forty shillings and costs under one summons, and costs in the remaining seven - £5.4s.6d.in all.' (7)

From these two reports we can see the incredible logic in which Dublin's ruler's dealt out justice. When one takes into consideration the Death Rate in Dublin and the incredible unsanitary conditions that prevailed one finds it inexplicable to find a person convicted of milk adulteration having their fine reduced from £100 to £10 while in a similar Court a week before a manager of a cinema had fines totalling £5.4s.6d. for allowing minors into the cinema unaccompanied by an adult. It seems that morality for the law custodians could somehow be divorced from the living conditions of the vast majority of Dublin's population. The overall feeling that one is confronted with in these social ills is paternalism, the good-works syndrome as portrayed in the report about the 'good ladies' who performed the work of mercy.

In 1900 the Lancet sent a Commissioner to investigate the sanitary conditions of the national schools of Dublin. Of one of the schools he wrote "Schoolrooms, dark and ill-ventilated; gas burning in the daytime; no recreation grounds, no bread from ten till two o'clock; no lavatory for the boys, manure heaps against the walls of school; dark brown liquid manure oozing from it forming stagnant pools, saturating unpaved porous ground, emanations into school garbage dust heaps, black mud, fish heads, offal etc, in the lanes and yards about."

In 1904 the Medical Officer of Health of the city of Dublin ordered his sanitary inspectors to investigate the sanitation of the national schools. Their report was embodied in a report of the state of public health for that year and shows that the general sanitary condition of the city schools was truly deplorable when it is remembered that habits of cleanliness or unseemliness contracted In childhood tend to root themselves in our natures it will be understood how great an influence for evil such a school environment must have been subjected to them.

Such reflections will help to explain the deplorable apathy of many of the tenants of the Dublin slums and their heartbreaking acquiescence in the continuance of conditions so destructive of the possibility of clean living. The report in question states the English Board of Education requirements in the line of sanitary accommodation for schools and the detailed reports of the Dublin inspectors show that the Dublin schools seldom reach one half of the amount necessary in the interest of health and decency.

In some schools as for instance St.Patrick's Lower Tyrone Street, having 244 pupils, attended by boys and girls, the W.C.s were opened to and used indiscriminately by boys and girls alike.

Sinn Fein, like the Church, never questioned the validity of a system which caused so much educational deprivation and yet many of the Sinn Feiners themselves were literate men engaged in teaching and journalism. The only reference to education in their fifteen point programme was number 11 'reform on national lines of education'. They shared with the Church the idea, which they both propagated, that the Anglican religion was the root cause of distress in the education system and the biggest danger was Protestantism. They could speak with some authority when pointing to the position of literacy and general education in Ulster (8). Sinn Fein would point to the success of the English propaganda when during the school children's' strike one of the demands was that the teaching of Irish be abandoned.

Chapter 6
Strike

T he rise of what can be described as the New Union Movement in England but with the addition of a paramilitary force was led by James Larkin. The decision to establish the Union on the quays of Dublin had been taken in the last week of December 1908.(1) The formal establishment of the Irish Transport and General Workers Union dates from January 4th 1909.(2)

By May 1910 when the Union had affiliated •to the Irish Congress its membership was 3,000; affiliation gave the I.T.W.U. the potential leading position inside the Labour Movement.(3) James Connolly had joined the Irish Transport Workers Union in 1911, as an organiser; by the time of the 1913 strike membership was at 12,000. The Irish Transport Workers sister union was led by James Larkin's own sister, Deliah, who founded the Irish Women Workers Union in 1911, whose operations soon extended to Belfast.(4) In the spring of 1912, the Irish Women Workers Union applied to the Irish TUC for affiliation and paid fees on some 1,000 members.(5) These figures remained constant after the 1913 Strike while those of the I.T.W.U. fell to 5,000. The combined membership of the Unions in 1913 was 13,000.

The employers were combined in an organisation of some 400 in Dublin.(5) It was Larkin who was seen as the figurehead and leader of the strike not only being the leader of the unskilled worker he was also a founder-member of the Irish Labour Party. In the January of 1912, Larkin was one of the seven candidates nominated by Labour (6), to stand in the local elections and despite the efforts of some of the employers and the Church through scurrilous propaganda to affect the result, five of the seven candidates were returned. Larkin's personal triumph was that he polled over 1,200 votes as against 500 for his opponent. Although this was only a drop in the political ocean, the total number of seats contested was eighty, it was still seen by many working people as a sign of radical change.

In November 1913, the Irish Citizens Army was founded, followed one month later by the Irish Volunteers. The Citizens Army was formed from the ranks of the labour movement led by Captain White, an Ulster Protestant, sympathetic to the cause of labour.

All sections of Dublin's population were represented in the Citizens' Army.(7) It achieved popular acclaim, but as soon as its nationalist rival, the Irish Volunteers, was launched, it immediately lost membership. Differences with the skilled and the unskilled, the white collar worker, and the small shop-keeper, the lack of proper facilities aggravated the problem.

There were also concerns about the politics of Larkin and O'Casey who despite the attacks from the TUC, Sinn Fein, the Catholic Church and the employers stuck to a hard socialist line, while Connolly and the Countess Markievicz wanted closer links with the Volunteers. Captain White stuck bravely to his post in trying to maintain a unified force but finally in 1914 he resigned from the job and leadership was taken over by James Larkin and subsequently Connolly.

Sinn Fein had been totally opposed to Larkin and the Unions, in 1908 during the Dublin Carters' Strike Arthur Griffith, the leader of

Sinn Fein, began to label Larkin "the strike organiser", and even after the Irish Transport Union was formed Griffith went on denouncing its activities as "English Trade Unionism".

In January 1909 Sinn Fein denounced as a monstrous state of affairs the fact that Irishmen should strike "without the sanction of the executive of the union".(8) This is a strange statement indeed when one considers the circumstances of the 1909 strike and who the executive of the union were. They were referring to the English executive of the National Union of Dock Labourers from which Larkin had recently been expelled and from whose ranks the members of the Irish Transport Workers Union came. Griffith had spent his life urging that Irishmen should disregard orders from England but when Irish trade unionists did this, he was the first to condemn them.

It was from this incident that Larkin's triumph in the local elections was dashed. He was disqualified from taking his seat because he was a convicted criminal. He had served three months of a twelve month hard labour sentence for criminal conspiracy and misappropriation of Dock Labourers' dues which Larkin had taken along with the poached members of that union.(9) Lord Askwith recalls the time when he heard Larkin "in one speech manage faithfully to pronounce equal criticism on The Government, the Catholic Church, The Pope, Ulster and the Salvation Army. No institution or person seemed to be safe from denudation".(10)

Larkin had a dislike for pseudo intellectuals; he would sometimes attend meetings of the Socialist Party of Ireland and denounce lecturers from the back of the hall.(11) Not that Larkin was without friends; his brother, Peter and himself were much respected in the United States where they had both worked with the I.W.W. Big Bill Hayward went to Dublin during the 1913 strike and was welcomed by

Larkin as was his help and advice. Larkin also enjoyed the support and encouragement of Tom Mann, Keir Hardie, George Lansbury, Victor Grayson, John Burns and that of Lenin.(12)

Whatever faults other politicians had found with him and no matter if he attacked everybody on the right and left he was still adored by the Dublin people,(13) and admired by his fellow trade unionists, for he had completed marathon tasks both in Belfast and in Dublin. In Belfast he had managed to unite Catholic and Protestant, and in Dublin he had done wonders with the unskilled, breaking down some of the barriers between the different social groups, inside the working class. When Larkin began his work in Dublin the skilled workers and their unions were inclined to regard his efforts with contempt,(4) mirroring the attitude shown to unskilled labour in England by the English skilled workers when the new unions were formed. One such skilled union, the Coach Maker, wrote to the Irish Worker "For many years we held to the old conservative ideas that we were a superior class of craftsmen. That coupled with religious dissension in our ranks, whereby somebody or other imagined they saw some ulterior motive behind any movement for the betterment of our conditions".(5)

It was the solidarity Larkin engendered between the skilled working people and the tenement dwellers that gave Larkin his great strength during the Strike. It worried the authorities, the Church and Sinn Fein that this man could lead and unite all sections of the working community, something they so far had failed to do.(13) (We must be careful when analysing people's political ideology. Skeffington was regarded by many as a socialist but judged the entirety of his political actions and his allies' one must judge him as a nationalist with socialist leanings.) (14)

Strike

During the early part of the summer of 1913 there were considerable indications of unrest in the city and county of Dublin. Between 1st January and 19th August 1913 there were 31 strikes involving 2,283 men and women and it appeared obvious as the months went by that a major confrontation was inevitable.(15)

The gauntlet was thrown down by the Directors of the Dublin United Tramways Company when they issued the following statement to the press: "The Directors are well aware of the attempts being made by James Larkin to foment disturbance among the men which, however, have met with little success. The Company have no apprehension of any trouble with their employees, and are prepared to meet any emergency that may arise" On Saturday, 27th July 1913 Mr. J. Murphy, owner of the Irish Independent, called a meeting of the employees of the Dublin Tramways Company, of which he was both chief shareholder and managing director. He warned his workers of the consequences of strike: "I want you to clearly understand that the directors of this company have not the slightest objection to the men forming a legitimate Union. And I would think there is talent enough amongst the men in the service to form a Union of their own, without allying themselves to a disreputable organisation, and placing themselves under the feet of an unscrupulous man who claims the right to give you the word of command and issue his orders to you and to use you as tools to make him the labour dictator of Dublin. ... I am here to tell you that this word of command will never be given, and if it is, that it will be the Waterloo of Mr. Larkin. A strike in the tramway would, no doubt, produce turmoil and disorder created by the roughs and looters, but what chance would the men without funds have in a contest with the Company who could and would spend £100,000 or more. You must recollect when dealing with a company of this kind that every one of the shareholders, to the number of five, six, or seven thousands, will have three meals a day whether the men succeed or not. I don't know if the men who go out can count on this."

On the 21st August, about 100 employees in the Tramways Company received a dismissal notice: "As the Directors of the Tramways Company understand that you are a member of the ITGWU whose methods are disorganising the trade and business of the city, they do not further require your service". On the same day the Directors discharged a hundred employees in the parcel department for being members of the Irish Transport Workers Union. A circular was given to employees by companies inside the Employers' Federation asking the men to state if they would by loyal to their employers or to the Unions. Several members in the dispatch department of the Independent newspaper were dismissed. A meeting was called by Larkin on the 23rd August of Tramway Company men who voted by 837 to 147 to strike.(16)

The threatened strike of the tramway men started on Tuesday 26th of August (Dublin's Horse Show Week) shortly before 10 o'clock when about two hundred men left their cars in the streets without any warning, that night there was a large meeting at Beresford Place addressed by William O'Brien (President of the Tailors' Society), James Larkin, Patrick Daly, Thomas Lawlor and William Partridge, all making inflammatory speeches.

Larkin, O'Brien, Daly, Lawlor and Partridge were arrested on warrants for charges of seditious speaking, conspiracy and several other similar complaints. They were released on bail; the case being held over until December. Partridge was twice arrested for making speeches which the judge himself admitted was peaceful. "I am sure", said Partridge, "that I will now be arrested if I publicly recite the Lord's Prayer".

The next night Larkin again addressed a large meeting announcing that at the meeting in Sackville Street on the following Sunday women and children should keep away; on the following night Larkin made another inflammatory speech advising people to hold their meetings in defiance of the police. Following this the Chief Magistrate issued a proclamation prohibiting the Sunday meeting. Larkin, addressing ten thousand people publicly burnt a copy of the proclamation, saying "I am going to burn the Proclamation of the King. I care as much for the King as I do for Swifte the Magistrate, People make Kings, and people can unmake them......I never said God save the King but in derision...." He also made the crowd repeat after him "I will not pay any rent until the tramway men have got the conditions they demand". (*) Note: Arising from this some Tramcar men were brought before the Court under the Tramways Bill, 1871, for leaving their cars unattended, and the response from the Union was not, as one would suppose, that of hardened syndicalists as many writers have tried to portray Larkin and his Union, but one of people following very much the conventional line on arbitration courts, they took the matter back to the Court pleading the Trades Dispute Act 1906 gave them immunity, and also quoted the Company Regulations concerning manning.(17)

Inflammatory speeches were also delivered by Connolly and Partridge. Following the speech by Larkin, a warrant was issued for his arrest. Larkin evaded the police until the following Sunday and was tried on the 27th October, sentenced to seven months, but released on the 13th November.

Partridge and Connolly were also arrested following their speeches. Partridge gave the required bail, which James Connolly refused to do. On the 30th August he was committed to jail for three months. He began a hunger strike on the 6th September and was released from prison on the 13th on his own recognisance.

The incident surrounding Larkin's arrest caused one of the worst riots in Dublin's history. A large crowd had gathered in Sackville Street on Sunday to see if Larkin would attend the meting. It seemed impossible as the area was cordoned off by Police, but Larkin had enlisted the aid of actress Helena Molony who helped disguise Larkin to look like an old man. This was done in the home of Countess Markievicz. Accompanied by his niece, Nellie Giffard, who did all the necessary talking, he drove up to the Imperial Hotel owned by Murphy and went to rooms which had been booked and had a balcony overlooking the street. Larkin began to address the crowd.(18) He was arrested, but the effect was electric. A riot followed, in which over a hundred people were arrested and over 400 civilians, including several women and girls were treated in hospital. There were fatalities: James Nolan and John Byrne, both through fractured skulls, and one other - that of Alice Brady who died of lock-jaw, after receiving a wound from a pistol fired by a scab labourer.(19)

The Lord Mayor demanded an immediate public inquiry into the general conduct of the police following the Beresford Place riot. But Mr. J. Murphy was so grateful to the police for their services that they were given the privilege of free rides on the trams (they retained this privilege until 1938). Murphy declared that he was ready to spend three-quarters of a million pounds to defeat the strike.

On September 1st, the biggest employer of female labour, W & R Jacob & Co Ltd., closed down part of their factory. On the same day the Tramway Works were closed down by Strikes. There was also serious rioting reported in the city. Tramway setts were being uprooted, and bottles and missiles were thrown from the houses at the police. One hundred persons were injured on this occasion. The damage to property was considerable, and on the 2nd September the Dublin Coal Merchants' Association decided to lock out the members of the Irish Transport Union, and on the 3rd September the employers federation issued the following statement: "That this meeting of employers, while asserting its friendly feelings to Trades Unionism, hereby declares that the position created by the Irish Transport and General Workers' Union (a Union in name only) is a menace to all trade organisation, and has become intolerable. That in order to deal effectively with the present situation all employers should bind themselves to adopt a common line of action by signing the agreement presented herewith." The agreement was that they, the employers, would not employ any person who was a member of the Irish Transport and General Workers' Union.

The Trade Union Congress opened on September 1st, in Manchester; delegates were listening to the President, Mr. W. J. Davis of the Brass Workers' Union, who was receiving the usual greetings when an urgent telegram from the Dublin Trades Council arrived asking for the right to speak to Congress which was agreed. They reported on the grave situation facing the workers in Dublin and so strong were their declarations that they were given an ovation and it was agreed a deputation from the TUC would go to Dublin immediately. Partridge, the chairman of the Dublin branch of the Engineers' Union related the acts of violence and outrage committed by the police in Dublin: "A young woman worker had just gone to bed when the police broke into her house. The girl hid in the closet. She was dragged out of there by the hair. These "men" beat up children." The Delegates passed the a resolution unanimously in support of the Dublin Strike, Ben Tillett declared "stand up to it!" amid loud cheers, most of the delegates rising to hold up their hands.(20) Such was the sectarianism of the General Council a call from the Gas workers to send a telegram giving support to the Cornish workers on strike with a condemnation of the violence shown by the police described as equal to that in Dublin was ruled out of order as the union in question "The Workers' Union" (lead by Tom Mann) was not affiliated.(20)

The TUC leadership wanted to keep Mann and his politics at arm's-length since his arrest in 1912 for inciting mutiny following an open letter to British soldiers titled 'Don't Shoot'; the letter was a plea for servicemen not to act against fellow workers, the letter was published by the Irish Worker. Decades later, when Mann was 75, he was sentenced to 18 months' hard labour for a similar offence in Ulster; the judge remarked, "A man of your age should know better", Mann retorted, "Sir, the older I get and the more I travel the world, the more I witness of the of exploitation of the working classes".

Speeches were delivered of a revolutionary kind that had not been heard for a long time. A resolution was moved to transfer the whole Congress to Dublin, and to organise a general strike throughout the whole of Great Britain. Smiley, the chairman of the Miners' Union, declared that the Dublin methods will compel all the workers to agree to Strike, and if needs be take up arms.(21)

The 5th September 1913 witnessed the first Trades Union Congress delegates arrive from England, William Brace, John Ward, and Jack Jones from the Congress, and A. J. Seddon, John Hill and Harry Gosling representing the Parliamentary Committee of the Congress.(22)

The TUC delegation soon got down to business, they had interviews immediately with the Lord Lieutenant, the Lord Mayor, the employers including Mr. Murphy, chairman of the Dublin Tramway Company, as well as with James Larkin and delegates representing workers on strike. In his autobiography, Harry Gosling states: "Jim Larkin, had adopted a highly aggressive policy of attacking employers individually and extending the use of the sympathetic strike, which meant the workers were continually refusing to handle what they called "tainted goods," and were thereby involving sections of the community so far untouched by the dispute." This policy was being met by the employers with an equally aggressive policy of the sympathetic lock-out. Gosling tried his best to cause divisions between Connolly and Larkin, stating to Connolly: "The leaders in the movement were obviously not playing the game. How could the people tolerate them?" Connolly's retort was: "You simply don't understand, Gosling". Gosling's delegation gave assurances to the employers that they would do everything possible to bring about a settlement to the Dublin dispute. They then had a series of sympathy meetings in Dublin on the theme of the right of free speech, and agreed to organise food ships to help the strikers and their families, who were destitute. The first food ships supplied by the English Trades Unionists arrived on the 27th September, and the total donations subscribed by supporters of the strikers came to £150,000. This came from all sections of the globe. In Great Britain the Miners' Federation alone subscribed £1,000 a week for several months.

The T.U.C. subscribed £5,000, the Parliamentary Committee and the 'Daily Citizen' contributed nearly £94,000 to the war chest, and 'The Daily Herald' also gave several thousands of pounds.(24) But although the British labour movement gave generously in an economic sense there was still much bad feeling in Dublin because of the lack of action in the way of sympathy strikes, such as the Dublin railwaymen had shown in 1911, with their solidarity strike in support of English railwaymen.

Not to say there were no sympathy strikes. Seven thousand railwaymen went out at Crewe, Sheffield, Derby, Liverpool and Birmingham,(1) and in London a magnificent meeting was held in Trafalgar Square, where groups of Socialists and workers came with their banners; there were many posters with cartoons and slogans on topical events, the crowd particularly applauded a poster which depicted a policeman waving a red flag bearing the inscription "Silence!"; the most prominent speakers were Tillett and Partridge, the chairman of the Dublin branch of the Engineers' Union.(23)

Sinn Fein first recognised the Transport Strike through its journal on September 6th 1913 with a front-page leader under the heading "Dublin Riots"..."with luxury and extravagancies flaunting themselves on all sides there are unplumbed depths of misery and sordid grinding poverty in every fetid court and alley in Dublin and other Irish cities. Want and disease in every crumbling tenement. Smoldering discontent and a sullen sense of enduring wrong shared by a large section of the population." The article goes on to blame the English: "Anglicanisation has spread like a canker in our cities"...."the richer folk have long been un-Irish in their sympathies and outlook but the poorer people and the middle class until quite recently were distinctively Irish in most things. The middle classes are still not too far gone on that road to denationalisation."

On September 13th, 1913 another full page article appeared in Sinn Fein's journal. After again blaming foreign rule for the troubles, Sinn Fein continues…"A national government would no doubt be able to hold the beam straight between capital and labour, but no national government is in being, and English industrial methods are in force in all of our big businesses,(24) our people are ill-paid, ill-fed, scandalously housed and in many cases overworked." The article goes on to support the right to join a trade union, condemns papers which on one hand condemn combination by labour but endorse it when applied to employers' federations. "Can the labour unrest be turned into national channels, and on the other hand can the condition of the labourers be improved by the Irish people themselves?"..."If they joined English Unions' amalgamated with English Parties and become further Anglicised the loss is Ireland's." Sinn Fein offers itself as the only party able to hold a beam straight between capital and labour, coupling this with Irish nationalist traditions, putting forward the proposition that all the problems which exist are simply manifestations of a corrupt imperialistic rule.

The food ships became an important weapon in the propaganda war launched by Sinn Fein against the labour movement pointing out how the Irish railway workers had rallied to support their English brothers when they had been in dispute in 1911 and how the only reciprocal action that could be offered by the English was charity. "The Englishmen, therefore, had a perfect right to send, not the money, but money's worth, if they so pleased. But let Irishmen understand the meaning of the transaction. Certain Englishmen subscribed £5,000 for the Irishmen who Want Out while they Stayed in. But if they had sent that £5,000 here in cash, England would have been the poorer by the Industry which £5,000 could stimulate. Therefore the English kept the cash, and with it stimulated English industry to the extent of £5,000, the product of which they gave to Ireland. Thus the actual cash has been kept in England and still remains in England circulating and stimulating English trade."

But each time Sinn Fein attacked the labour movement it had to offer an alternative to the mass of poor people who inhabited the town and country of Ireland. It realised only with popular mass support could its objectives be realised.(25)

The Church and Sinn Fein were in unison during the strike over a major social issue which involved children. This was when the idea of evacuating children of the strikers who were suffering hardship to England for the duration of the strike was proposed. Archbishop Walsh was uncompromising in his opposition to the scheme and launched a counter-movement which was subsequently successful in stopping the evacuation. Dr Walsh, the Bishop of Dublin, went so far as to write a letter of protest against the proposal to send the children to England. He said "Catholic mothers no longer will be worthy of the name if they so far forget themselves as to send their children to be cared for in a strange land without any security that: those to whom the children are handed over are Catholic or persons of any faith at all".

The Dublin working class were polarised, they had to decide whether to abide by the Church, something that was deep-rooted in their psyche, or fight for a better life through the labour movement. This was brought to the fore following the decision to evacuate the poorest children whose families were on strike or were being locked-out in some cases to save them from near starvation and the subsequent illnesses that they were all too familiar with. The scheme was masterminded, as was the general welfare program, by Deliah Larkin.

There were many suffragettes prominent, but apart from one or two exceptions such as Countess Markievicz and Mrs. Skiffington most were of either English or American extraction. The Irish suffragette movement almost completely ignored this incident as it did the whole of the labour unrest.

There were many remarkable scenes in Dublin. One occurred in Kingstown when several priests prevented the departure of nineteen boys for England, when Mrs. Rand and Mrs. Ward, despite the protests of the priests succeeded in getting the children as far as Kingstown where a ship was waiting for them, but the Priests finally dissuaded the youngsters from sailing. One priest, boarding the ship and addressing the passengers, said the boys were being taken away by trickery and fraud and corruption and without the permission of their parents.(26) Arising from this the Countess Plunkett brought an action against Mrs. Rand, and later Mrs. Montefiore, who were arrested on a charge of taking away a boy named George Burke from the custody of his father without his father's consent. The boy alleged a woman, not the accused, told him they were going away for a week's holiday, and that when they came back they were to get some money. The boy's father also added that he gave nobody authority to take his son away.(27&28) Clearly this case was contrived, although the mother had given the authority she was rather conspicuous by her absence and was never asked to appear in Court or give a statement to the police. Mrs. Rand was a twenty-one year old American citizen, a catholic and a member of one of the wealthiest families in California The case caused quite a sensation in America and pressure was brought to bear both in the English and American press, and the Attorney General for Ireland dropped the case. There was much interest in America especially amongst the Irish Americans who were equally divided as to the rights and wrongs of the affair.(29)

It must have come as a deep shock to the Dublin working class when the Church, who had been their paternal benefactor, suddenly rejected them and ignored their very real plight. For the first time in their lives hundreds of Irish mothers who had been the back-bone of the Church were forced into this position of accepting or rejecting the Church's edict. This must have left its mark on the ideology and faith of the mothers of Dublin who had accepted so much in the past and never blamed the Church, but always sought its sanctuary as protector. Given the hitherto subservient Dublin flock one can imagine the consternation when the following incidents occurred:

"A number of boys connected with the Pro-Cathedral Schools, Rutland Street, went on strike yesterday, damaged the schools, and prevented some of the pupils attending. "We want shorter hours like our fathers." was the reply which some of the urchins gave when questioned as to their conduct. About 12 of them picketed the school doors and prevented other pupils going to school. (30&31) Some of the windows were broken, and it is alleged that one of the teachers was wounded by a missile thrown through a window. Their demands, they said, were for shorter school hours, teaching of Irish to be abandoned, a half-holiday on Wednesday in addition to the Saturday half-holiday, school books to be supplied free, refusing to write on copy-books made by any firm involved in trade disputes." (32)

One of the clergymen of the Pro-Cathedral parish told an "Irish Independent" representative that the affair was very much exaggerated. "A few little brats of the street-Arab sort", he said, "tried to interfere with the boys to prevent them going to school this morning. One or two small windows were broken. All the girls attended school, and all the senior boys' classes were held as usual. I spoke to the parents of the urchins who were creating the mischief, and they promised they would give them a sound thrashing, and take care to make them go to school tomorrow."(33) The little barefoot urchins, boys and girls more daring than their elders ¬rushed out every now and then and gathered up fresh stones of ammunition for the mob. Darting out into the street, they had little trouble in finding plenty of broken bottles and bricks which had been used on the police a moment before. These missiles were again soon in use, and other youngsters and friends from the Tyrone Street side kept the mob supplied from here with missiles for the firing line. (34)

The Church's concern over the children was, I feel, genuine in the contents of it's' ideology "Saving Souls". It felt socialism to be almost the doctrine of the anti-Christ; viewing the act of feeding a thousand children per day at Liberty Hall by the Countess Markievicz not as a work of Christian Charity, but one of socialist enticement. (35) Haunted always by the Ne Tempere decree, as of course the Church was not in unison over the new theories, (although no public statements were ever made by members of the Church) there was some feeling that the deportation issue was an expression by some rebels of the unease felt by the flock, who in the true traditions of Irish Catholicism still remain loyal after this incident as they had done so many times before. (This most important religious development of the period had been the activation of the Ne Temere Papal Decree against mixed marriages in 1908, and the activation of the Motu Proprio Decree forbidding Catholics on pain of automatic excommunication, to bring civil or' religious charges against the Catholic clergy without the permission of the Catholic hierarchy, or to participate in any way (as judges, solicitors, etc) in cases resulting from such charges. The Ne

Temere decree declares that mixed marriages are unlawful unless they take place in a Catholic Church and unless the non-Catholic party signs a pledge that the children will be brought up as Catholics. Existing mixed marriages were declared invalid).

Another amusing incident is accounted in Fred Bower's "The Rolling Stonemason" when he recalls how he met a party of evacuees who had just arrived from Dublin at Liverpool, most of them ill-clad and barefoot. He was stopped by a priest and after an argument threatened to call the police which eventually he did, and after showing the authorities written consent given by the parents, the priest's attitude changed and the priest asked if he minded posing with the priest and the children for a photographer. The photograph was taken but when it appeared in the paper it appeared minus Fred Bower, with the caption "Children being taken to palatial foster homes in the charge of Father Walsh of Liverpool". (36) Bower also remarked on the fact that when the children did go back some three months later their appearances had so changed for the better that he hardly recognised them, but the number of children that did get through was small and in the end Deliah Larkin, the Women's Leader had to concede to the Church. This was a defeat for the social rebellion of the Dublin working community.

Sinn Fein used this opportunity both to back the Church and attack the Labour movement. "There are over 300 children in the slums of Sheffield here, wanting food and clothes. In God's name how can those people of those English ladies in Dublin say that the children would be sent to Catholic Schools? When the English are doing their very best to close our schools. Besides, English poor children are much worse off then the Irish poor children. Anyone may see this by going through Liverpool, Manchester, Sheffield and Leeds".(37) Sinn Fein, through statements such as this, united with the Church. The Church and Sinn Fein found a union perhaps based on mutual opposition to a subject they disliked for different reasons, but unite they did and they found that they could live with one another and that basically they had certain ideals which could unite them. The social implications were that the nationalist movement, Sinn Fein, though small, had an ally though perhaps not in a material sense but more a moralistic one which, when one considers the framework of both the ideology of Sinn Fein and the Catholic Church is an all-important one.

On the 12th September a large number of farmers of the County of Dublin decided to lock out their employees who belonged to the union. The Carters Association acted likewise and by Monday, 15th September, the day when the building trade employers locked out their employees who were members of The Transport union, the number of people locked out throughout the strike was about 8,000.

The numbers of people injured in riots in Dublin in 1913 was 479, far outstripping the total of 124 injured in the unrest of 1911 (which was claimed by the authorities to be unparalleled). (38)

The situation in Dublin worsened daily as the number of people out grew and the instances of civil unrest increased as the streets became filled with strikers and the victims of lockout. Business in the city was coming to a standstill and in the country practically all farm work had stopped and serious rioting occurred on the outskirts of Dublin. A public house was attacked in the village of Finglas, and one of the attackers was shot and wounded by a police officer. The story was the same in the city and several times the police batten-charged groups of workers, loose in the city and by 22nd September the number of people unemployed was estimated to be 20,000. When the families of these workers were included a total of 100,000, or one in four, in the city of Dublin were affected. (39) The situation inside the city had been worsened when a tenement block literally collapsed, seven people being killed and many more injured. The affect of this was so traumatic that Murphy's paper attacked the attitude of the tenement landlords. This article must have been sanctioned by Murphy himself who was one of Dublin's leading landlords. The army was used for emergency supplies to hospitals, etc. but there were no clashes with the strikers Sir George Askwith was brought in as mediator in late September (40) but even the greatest of industrial peacemakers found the situation almost impossible. There was an open enquiry headed by Askwith in which both sides of the dispute could give evidence in public but the court found itself unable to devise a remedy for the difficult situation, and negotiations were broken off between management and labour.(41&42)

Despite assistance in the form of food ships and funds from supporters from the British labour movement, and despite the resolution in support of the Dublin Strike at the TUC conference in Manchester in early September, the unofficial sympathy strikes in England were soon stopped when pressure was applied by the British Unions. This attitude was continued and made public at the special conference held in London in December. (43) The T.U.C special conference (Dublin Dispute) was convened on December 9th at the Memorial Hall London. Delegates to conference were not elected but selected. The Conference opened with a report from the delegation sent to Dublin to negotiate a settlement with the employers. Larkin immediately began heckling Arthur Henderson who was giving the report back alleging that the T.U.C. had tried to settle behind the Irish Transport Workers' back. Uproar followed. An uneasy peace was brought by Connolly and Harry Gosling, who both spoke in a conciliatory tone. Then a resolution of confidence was put to conference. It read "...the unfair attacks made by men inside the Trade Union Movement upon British Trade Union officials... it affirms its confidence in those officials who had been so unjustly assailed and its belief in their ability to negotiate an honourable settlement if assured of the effective support of all who have are concerned in the Dublin dispute". It was moved by Ben Tillett and seconded by W.C Anderson. (44) This was backed by Havelock Wilson, who attacked Larkin personally "Mr. Larkin had made great blunders from the inception, and carried them right to the end. The state of affairs in Dublin would not have existed for 24 hours had he shown a little common sense." (45) Larkin then spoke "Mr. Chairman and human beings." The hall was then in uproar. Larkin retorted "If you are not going to give me an opportunity of replying to these foul lying statements it would only be what I would expect from a good many of you"..."your money is useful, but money never won a strike"..."you could win the Dublin strike tomorrow if you meant it. If you don't mean it, shut up!"...."but we will never give in." (46) Tillett's motion was carried with only six delegates against. The conference then agreed to give financial support and act as mediator.

A resolution calling for a national strike was moved by Councillor Jack Jones and seconded by SJ Davis: "That this special congress having considered the report of the parliamentary committee on the Dublin dispute, whilst fully appreciating the efforts already made to bring the dispute to an end and the generous response made to the appeal of the parliamentary committee for funds hitherto resolves that further action is necessary to uphold the right of combination and to resist the attempts of the Dublin employers to oppose the transport workers union. We therefore call upon all Unions having members engaged in transport work either on land or sea, to notify their employers concerned that on a given date they will refuse to handle black leg cargo or merchandise going to or coming from firms which have locked-out the workers of Dublin. We call upon all Unions, not connected with the transport trades to pledge themselves to support, financially, by a fixed monthly levy, all workers who may be affected by the carrying out of the above proposed policy. We are also determined that the government shall immediately withdraw all extra military and police assistance being rendered to the Dublin employers in order that the above proposals may be carried into effect. This congress resolved that a special emergency committee of six be selected to act in conjunction with a Joint board so that all necessary steps may be taken to make the decision effective." This was defeated by 2,280,000 votes to 203,000....(47)

The action of this Congress was a far cry indeed from the fighting talk of the previous Trade Union Congress held only four months before: when Ben Tillett had urged in regard to Dublin "workers should have in mind their right to arm"; and from the Miners' delegate who had stated that they "would down tools in every corner of this country in a day or two, to give this matter (Dublin) consideration." (48) Robert Smiley, by the December conference, had also forgotten his words "that we will 'defend the interests of their people (Dublin's) by calling a conference and declaring a stoppage of labour all over the country",(49) which had been greeted by loud cheers. Only Jack Jones of the gas workers had stayed consistent. (50)

The TUC parliamentary committee now made it their business to try to isolate Larkin and Connolly. They talked directly to the employers and at every given opportunity they denounced the leadership of the strike. Sexton tried in vain to get members of the Irish Transport Workers Union to join his own discredited union.

Without sympathetic action the strike was doomed to failure as many of the unions in Ireland were either directly or indirectly controlled from England. The Irish labour movement simply didn't have the funds to feed the thousands who were now destitute. James Connolly wrote: 'And so we Irish workers must go down into Hell, bow our backs to the lash of the slave drive and eat the dust of defeat and betrayal.'

Early In January, as a result of a combined ballot of Dockers, seamen and firemen, former employees of the City of Dublin Steam Packet Company, it was decided by a large majority to resume work, and as the weeks went by more and more workers returned to work. The final blow to the unions came on the 19th January when between five and six hundred men, members of the Irish Transport Workers' Union, former employees of the City of Dublin, Silloth and Isle of Man Steamers, and the Duke Shipping Company, resumed work unconditionally. The end of the month virtually saw the end of the strike.

In Glasgow at a public meeting on January 31st, 1914 James Larkin admitted defeat. (51) This is not to say that all the participants in the lock out and strikes were taken back, and those that did not had to go back on the best terms that they could arrange for themselves. (52) Liberty Hall was like an empty shell. Workers were now afraid to identify themselves with the union. Financially as well as spiritually the Labour Movement was at its worst.

Larkin, a broken man, left for America in October, but his sister Deliah, who still controlled the country areas, launched an attack on Connolly and he `was compelled to suffer the venomous personal abuse of Miss Larkin's followers who missed no opportunity of vilifying him in the streets of Dublin'. Deliah had been asked to leave Liberty Hall with the Irish Women Workers Union because of the antagonism between herself and Connolly's followers. James Larkin, in an attempt at unity, agreed to the request. There was much criticism levelled at Deliah Larkin for the amount of money spent in Croydon Park on a house and land, which was used for social functions for the strikers and later the formation of the Citizens Army.

Some idea of the popularity of Deliah Larkin, who, along with the Jacobs' factory girls, had ran relief kitchens and the general welfare operations during the strike can be ascertained by an opinion poll on the subject of the most popular woman in the National Movement. Ms. Larkin, who clearly was not a supporter of Sinn Fein or any other extreme nationalist organisation, won by a large majority. Deliah, for a short time, published an anti-nationalist paper, on the old Irish Worker lines, called 'The Red Hand', although her brother James cabled from America for this to cease which it did.

All attempts to save the union failed and finally Larkin was vilified in America, England and indeed Ireland as a communist.

The Citizens Army was a mere shell. The Volunteer Army soon became the workers choice. Sinn Fein now used the pending defeat of the strike as propaganda weapon, denouncing strikes as a disease: "The sentiment of Patriotism, like that of religion has its origin in the very nature of things" and "the workers' disease known as the strike fever or the characteristic weakness of labour bodies for developing a sudden affection for idleness'.

Lenin commented "at the present moment the Irish nationalists (i.e., the Irish bourgeoisie) are the victors"

In America, having become active in the International Workers of the World movement, and having been a delegate to the founding convention of the American Communist Party, James Larkin was arrested and imprisoned for his political activities. He denounced the Anglo-Irish Treaty from his prison cell. James Larkin was deported and, when back in Ireland, in 1923 the union split officially. James Larkin then formed the Irish Workers Union.

James Connolly took up the post of Acting General Secretary to the Irish Transport and General Workers Union in 1915. He lead the socialist section in the uprising of 1916 where he was wounded. Subsequently he was tried by a military tribunal, sentenced to death, still suffering from his wounds, he was tied to a chair and shot by firing squad. The labour movement lost not only a great activist but a prolific writer and theoretician of great stature. The British Intelligence Papers demonstrate the danger Connolly was to the State, not only in Britain but also in America where Connolly had been very active with the Wobbles being a full-time officer and agitator for the Industrial Workers of the World (IWW) union.

In the First World War Murphy, mirroring the actions of Tillet & Co, acted as a recruiting sergeant for the British army; suggesting to fellow employers that they sack able-bodied men who did not enlist.
Sinn Fein gave the opportunity for the defeated labour movement to save face by blaming the English Labour Movement, and, by implication, Socialism. Grievances were still real but Labour now had a new champion who was allied with the Church. There was a falling-back to traditional enemies and heroes.

The Church felt at ease. The strain on the faith had been immense. They too could fall back into their traditional role as paternal godfather watching over the flock, guarding them from the alien enemy, Socialism.

Conclusion

T he six-month strike and lockout brought open rebellion to the surface, and during these months the political and social institutions were tested and challenged to the full including even the seemingly intractable social union of the Roman Catholic Church, and its' greatest adherents, the working class of Dublin.

Sinn Fein were the obvious political victors, although the Labour Movement was to play a significant role in the 1916 Easter Rising. Sinn Fein were the dominant political force and the Socialist Left was never able to recapture the ground lost during this period. Sinn Fein would use the nationalist card when challenged on their lack of solidarity with Irish workers, pointing to the betrayal of Larkin and the strikers by the 'English' T.U.C.

If the rebellion 1916 had been led by socialists with a proclamation calling for a Social State, what would the outcome in terms of history have been and what would the composition of the Republic in 1921 have been? One can only speculate.

I believe it would have acted as a catalyst to the movement on the mainland of Britain if the left had prevailed during the Dublin dispute and the right-wing of the T.U.C, especially the parliamentary committee, had been defeated. What would have been the attitude of organised labour and the Labour Representation Committee (Labour Party) towards the First World War? We know that their victory in

1913 only drove them further to the right, hardening attitudes towards Labour leaders like James Larkin and Tom Mann.

The T.U.C's actions did not just affect the Dublin working class but that of the rest of the United Kingdom. They had demonstrated, even at this early date, that a general strike in support of any section of workers, no matter what their predicament, was a thing to be avoided at all costs - agitation was now to be replaced by conciliation. They were now indeed 'respectable' members of the working class. The role of the T.U.C was firstly to maintain the dominance of the right and at all costs to deal with supporters, agitators, fellow-travellers and others and all perceived enemies from within.

The success and the very existence of a left within the British trade union structure is owed to the perseverance of Socialists like Tom Mann and the organisational framework and discipline masterminded by theoreticians versed in both in theory and practice who devised a strategy to remove industrial power away from the bureaucracy to the membership through the Shop Stewards Movement, such as those that existed in industry - the print, mines and the docks. Until the early seventies this ideology was based on the analysis of the reality of the British labour movement as it really existed and not how some would like it be.

Larkin and Connolly could not have got so far in 1913 unless they had won the hearts and minds of the working class of Dublin - a lesson which unfortunately has never been fully understood and appreciated.

Bibliography

Reports and Commissions

Report Commission XIX DH 1913 Report Commission XIV 1914 Report Commission XVIII 1914 .1911 Census. Report Commissioners, Dublin Hospital, Housing Enquiry 1914 XIV...Board of Trade Report (Ed 6955) 1913 .Irish TUC Report 1912 .Review Ireland Review XXXII 1910 .Dublin Disturbances Commission 1914.Parliamentary Papers XVIII CCD 7269.Special Report   Dublin Schools, Lancet 1901.British Intelligence Reports 1913-16 .TUC Special Report on Dublin 1914 .TUC Report 1913 NUDL.ReportTom Mann Papers Surveys. William Booth. Conversations with George Woodcock, Jenny Tillett, J.P Miller. Walter.Southgate.and   Walter   Citrine   .Newspapers   The   Irish Independent .The Irish Times. New York Times .The Irish Citizen .Sinn Fein .The Irish Catholic .Irish Worker .Daily Herald .The Freeman's Journal

Chapter 1

Labour and Capital

(1) Essays in labour history, G D.H.Cole (2) History of the Irish Working Class, P.B.Ellis (3) K. Marx on Ireland (4) History of the Irish Working Class, P.B.Ellis (5) Ibid 6 (See the Currah Mutiny 1914) (6) The

age of Empire, E Hobsbawn (7) Essays in labour history, G D.H.Cole "Marx to Kugelmann (8) Engel's Letters to Marx (9) Stevedores and Dockers, Lovell (10) Dock Strike 1889 T. McCarthy (11) Popes new order P.Huhges. (12)William Booth Surveys

Chapter 2

Labour v. Labour

(1) Up and Down Stream Harry Gosling (2) George Lansbury R. Postgate (3) Keir Hardie, Kenneth O Morgon (4) Essays in labour history, G D.H.Cole (5) Walter Southgate The way it was, T. Philpot (6) Interviews with. Jenny Tillett (7) Victor Grayson, David Clark See Ben Tillet.Jonathan Schemer J.Gorman Images of Labour

Chapter 3

Sinn Fein and the Church

(1-2)What Sinn Fein stands for" A.De Blacan (3-5) Sinn Fein The Daily Herald (6) - (7)the Irish Independent The Newspaper (8)Catholic Political Culture Gannon (9) Irish Catholic The Newspaper (10-11) James Larkin E Larkin (12) B.Gitlow The Whole of there lives(13) -15) Connolly and Partition, B. & I.C.(16)Fiery Cross .Deasy

Chapter 4

Right v. Left   Sexton and Larkin

(1)Stevedores and Dockers. Lovell (2) The Dockers Union Taplin (3) TUC Report 1913 (4) JP Miller's history of the L.C.M not the TUC edited edition (5) Larkin by Fox (6) Victor Grayson, David Clark (7)

Tom Mann papers Tom Mann (8). Larkin, James Larkin (9) NUDL Executive Reports (10) conversations with George Woodcock former general-secretary of the TUC and a leading member of Catholic Action

Chapter 5

Dublin

(1) Housing Enquiry 1914 XIV,also Lancet Commission 1900 (2) Dublin Disturbances Commission 1914, Parliamentary Papers XVIII CCD 7269 (3) The 1911 Census (4) The Irish Independent (5) Fifty Years of Liberty Hall" I.T.W.U, Also from the many interviewees, kindly introduced to me by the IT.W.Union Exploitation also (Appendix housing and cost of living) (6) Report Public Health Committee also Report commissioners, Dublin Hospital (7) The Irish Independent (8) Sinn Fein Newspaper

Chapter 6

Strike

(1) Fifty Years of Liberty Hall. I.T.W.U. pp.30 (2) T.U.C. SIR 1914 (3) James Larkin by Emmet Larkin pp.96 (4) Report of the Irish T.U.C. 1912 (5) British Intelligence Papers& (5).Irish Worker (6) James Larkin by Emmet Larkin pp.89 (7) The Irish Worker, 20th January 1912. There are several books and pamphlets on Larkin, the best I believe being: James Larkin by Emmett Larkin, slightly biased in favour of Larkin, but undoubtedly the best researched and most accurate (7) "History of the Irish Working Class", B.Ellis (8) Sinn Fein Newspaper (9) The Dockers Union E .Taplin (10) Lord Asquith Industrial Problems and Disputes.'(11)Larkin' by Fox See James Larkin Emmett Larkin (12) Lenin on Britain (13) Larkin by Fox The Wobbles P. Renshaw,).Ibid\

"Industrial Problems Askwith 'Larkin' Fox pp. Irish Worker, (15) Reports Commissions XVIII pp 430 (16) British Intelligence Notes Note I have taken as my source for the strike the Intelligence Notes (17) Jim Larkin by Fox, 1 See B.I.N. for speeches and account. (18) Fox by Larkin (19) British Intelligence.Notes. For accounts and speeches see also Daily Herald, 3rd Jan. 1914 for report. (20) TUC Report. (21)Lenin British Labour (22) Harry Gosling Up and down stream and T.U.C. Conference Report 19139(23) Lenin Class war in Dublin. (24)Daily Herald (25) Sinn Fein Newspaper. (26) "The Rolling Stonemason." Fred Bower (27) See "What Sinn Fein Stands for" A E Blacan (28) Larkin by Larkin (29) New York Times, 23rd October 1913 (Desmond Greave's Life of Connolly for good descriptions. (30) New York Times, (31) The Irish Citizen (32&33) Irish Independent, (34) "The Rolling Stonemason." Fred Bower (35) Irish Independent New York Times,) (36) Fred Bower's "The Rolling Stonemason (37) 'Sinn Fein' See Appendix Strikers Received at Hospitals (39 Irish Independent 1st Sept 1913 See B. 1. N •) (40) Sir George Askwith Problems and Disputes (41) British Intelligence Notes (42) New York Times (43) (Daily Citizen and The Daily Herald) (44) The Daily Herald 10/12/13 (45) The Freeman's Journal (46) 1914 TUC. Report on Conference (47) Ibid (48) British Intelligence Notes (49) Fifty Years of Liberty Hall, I.T.W (50) Special TUC.Congress on Dublin Report 1914 (51) Freeman's Journal (52) British Intelligence Notes

Appendix

LEO XIII RERUM NOVARUM 151

Workers and Employer's

One of the Church's most useful functions is to prevent the ever recurring strife, by reminding each class of its duties to the other, and especially of the obligations of justice.

What are these Obligations?

For the Workers they are: to carry out honestly and fairly all equitable agreements freely entered into; never to injure an employer's property or his person; never to resort .to violence in defending their own cause, or to riots or disorder; to shun evil-principled agitators.

For the wealthy Owner and Employer, the obligations are: not to consider workmen as bondsmen; to respect the worker's dignity as a man and as a Christian; to remember that it is shameful and inhuman to treat men like chattels to make money by, or to look upon them merely as so much muscle and physical strength; to remember the needs of the worker's soul, provide time and opportunity for his religious duties, and guard him from dangerous occasions of sin in his work; never to tax the workers beyond their strength, or to employ them in work unsuited to their sex or age but above all else, the employer's great and principal duty is to give everyone what is just in this matter of wages; to exercise pressure upon the needy and the destitute for the sake of gain, to gather one's profit out of another's need is condemned by all laws, human and divine; to defraud anyone of his due wages is a sin that cries to Heaven for vengeance, hence the employer is bound to refrain, religiously, from cutting down wages whether by force, by fraud or by usurious dealing.

The Church reminds both that they are, equally, the children of God, equally in need of the Redemption. The Pope warns the rich that wealth is no passport to eternal happiness, but is rather a hindrance, and says that the rich should tremble at the threatening of Jesus Christ-threatening so unwonted in the mouth of Our Lord ' and remember that one day they must strictly account to God for all their wealth.

Wages, Rent and Retail Prices

DUBLIN: Summary - Wages, Rent and Retail Prices 1 Report of the Board of Trade Ed 6955 (Cost of Living of the Working Classes 1913)

Report Commissioners, Dublin, Hospital Housing Enquiry 1914 XIV

Trade Union Rate of Wages:
Where the rate of wages is per hour, the week usually consists of 54 hours

Bakers and Confectioners	36s per week
Boiler Makers	38s per week
Bookbinders	33s per week
Brass Founders & Gasfitters	33s per week
Brick and Stone Layers	9d per hour

Appendix

Butchers	32s per week
Carpenters (Amalgamated)	9d per hour
Coach makers	28s to 40s per week
Coopers	36s per week upwards
Corporation Labourers	28s per week (average)
Irish Drapers' Assistants	20s per week upwards
Irish Transport Workers	25s to 28s per week
Iron founders	30s per week
Litho. Artists and Engravers	36s to 40s per week
Painters	34s per week (av)
Plasterers	9d per hour
Plumbers	9d per hour
Poulterers	28s-30s per week
Printers, (Typo)	30s per week
Saddlers	30s per week
Shipwrights	36s to 38s per week
Smiths	30s per week
Stereotypers	36s per week
Tinsmiths and Sheet Metal Workers	30s-50s per week

Compared in 1905 and 1912, percentage Increase (+) or Decrease (-) in rents and retail prices combined:

London	Wales & Monmouth	Scotland	Ireland
+8.5	+12.9	+10.9	+12.2

Predominant rate of wages 1912:

	London		Dublin		Edinburgh	
	Skilled/Labourer		Skilled/Labourer		Skilled/Labourer	
Bricklayers and Masons	10½d	7d	8½d	4¾d	9½d	5½d
Carpenters and Joiners	11d	-	8 or 8½d	-	9½d	-
Painters	8½ or 9d	-	7½ or 8d	-	9d	-
Plumbers and Plasterers	11d	7d	8 or 8½d	-	9d	-
Compositors	39 s per week	-	35 s per week	-	34 s per week	-

Rate of wages compared with London 1912:

	Skilled	Labourer	Compositor
Wales & Monmouth	84.8	84. 8	86,5
Scotland	85.6	79.1	85.6
Ireland	72.3	53.7	84.2

Dublin, summary of wages, rent and retail prices:

	Percentage Increase (+) or Decrease (-) (compared 1905/1912)	Index numbers compared with London = 100
Rates of wages:		
Building - Skilled	+2	79
Building - Labourers	+6	66
Printing - Compositors	nil	90
Rents (including rates):	nil	75
Food - Meat	-2	78
Food - Other	+11	107
Total Food	+8	99
Coal	+17	85
Total Food and Coal	+9	97
Rent and Retail Prices combined	+7	93

Wage rates comparison with London taking the index at 100:

	Builders	Builders' labourers	Engineers	Engineers' labourers	Printers
Belfast	81	56	98	73	90
Cork	76	61	85	72	88
Dublin	79	66			90
Limerick	67	50			79
Derry	66	46			74
Waterford	65	43			

Industrial disputes 1900-1914

	Working days lost	Number of stoppages	Workers involved
1900	3,088	633	185
1901	4,130	631	179
1902	3,438	432	255
1903	2.320	380	116
1904	1,464	346	87
1905	2,368	349	92
1906	3,019	479	218
1907	2,148	585	146
1908	10,785	389	293
1909	2,678	422	297
1910	9,867	521	514
1911	10,155	872	952
1912	40,890	834	1,462
1913	9,804	1,459	664
1914	9,807	972	447

Strikers Received at Dublin Hospitals

	1911	1913
Jervis Street	98	320
Mecer	14	50
Meooth	9	26
Steevens	3	20
St Patrick's	0	63
Total	124	479
Police Injured	22	57

Appendix

Housing

Report Commission XIX Dublin Hospital Inquiry 1913 also from XIX p XV Vol VII Census for England and Wales 1911

As to the rents that were paid they were variable, but a guide can be taken from the **rents charged in municipal housing**:

Weekly family income		Rent	
50/-	8/-	to	10/-
40/-	6/-	to	8/-
30/-	4/6	to	6/-
25/-	4/-	to	5/-
20/-	3/-	to	4/-
15/-	1/6	to	2/-
10/-	1/-	to	1/6

Number of rooms per tenement:

	Dublin	Glasgow	Belfast	Liverpool	London	Manchester	Birmingham
(1)	339	200	6	54	134	18	10
(2)	210	462	41	74	190	35	21
(3)	105	189	50	132	213	97	305
(4)	104	66	239	185	159	406	165

Average number of occupants per room in tenements of 1 room, 2 rooms, 3 rooms and 4 rooms:

	Dublin	Glasgow	Belfast	Liverpool	London	Manchester	Birmingham
(1)	3.31	3.18	2.23	2.09	1.92	1.79	1.69

(2)	2.26	2.43	1.59	1.68	1.71	1.49	1.39
(3)	1.64	1.73	1.40	1.51	1.37	1.39	1.43
(4)	1.29	1.25	1.70	1.15	1.19	1.09	1.10

Number of Persons per 1,000 total population living in tenements of 1 room, 2 rooms, 3 rooms and 4 rooms:

	Dublin	Glasgow	Belfast	Liverpool	London	Manchester	Birmingham
(1)	229	132	3	23	59	7	3
(2)	194	496	26	50	149	22	26
(3)	106	205	42	122	200	86	42
(4)	110	69	223	173	174	376	223

Dublin Tuberculosis Death Rate

	1908	1909	1910	1911	1912
Independent Class	73	63	149	115	41
Middle Class	223	236	242	235	192
Artisan Class & Petty Shopkeepers	371	294	271	304	294
General Service Class	339	369	355	356	316
Domestic Servants	132	131	161	172	183

While there has been a slight reduction in the death rate in Dublin from all causes in recent years, still the death rate for the year 1911, the last year for which complete returns are available for the United Kingdom, was higher than in any of the large centres of population in England, Wales, Scotland and we fear until the housing problem is adequately dealt with no substantial reduction in the death rate may be hoped for. (1)

(1) Report Commissioners Dublin Hospital Housing Enquiry 1914 XIV

The Church and Children

The Catholic Church in Dublin supplied 25,451 meals to Catholic Primary school children this number included the 1,589 who were fully boarded by the Church

The Irish Catholic 7th June 1913

Walter Southgate

Socialist

Walter Southgate was the quintessential rank-and-file activist born in East London in 1890 of working-class parents.

Walter enjoyed the comforts of a typical east London two-up, two-down cottage. He excelled at school and should have gone into further education, but the financial situation at home ensured that he left school at 14.

Although Walter's parents had no funds for him to be indentured into one the arts and crafts trades, he found employment as a junior clerk in a solicitor's office and soon mastered the intricacies of the legal profession, especially trade union and Labour law. When his employer asked if he wanted to be a solicitor, in typical Southgate fashion he answered 'both you and I know I haven't the money and I come from the wrong class'.

He used his legal skills when he took up employment with the National Union of Clark's - he was their delegate to Hackney Trades Council. Walter was then a member of Hyman's Marxist Social Democratic Federation. Through his Trades Council, he was a delegate to the Labour Representation Committee.

Walter Southgate was a lover of the outdoors and was instrumental in forming the Hackney branch of the Clarion Cycle Club. Both his skills as a graphic artist and writer were used by the Clarion movement. Walter was the author and compiler of the Clarion year-book and designed leaflets, posters and other art propaganda for the movement until the First World War.

Walter, like many Socialists, saw the First World War as an imperialist war and refused to fight. Famously, when the magistrate from the tribunal cross-examined Walter on why he wouldn't fight, asking 'didn't he want to defend his home?' Walter answered that 'the Kaiser must be really hard-up if he wants my house!' Walter than went on the trot, working where he could in the country, keeping his head down throughout the war years.

In 1920 became clerk to the Sheet Metal Workers Union a post which he held until 1943.

Walter continued to be an active Socialist, writing many articles for the socialist press and acting as secretary to his Trades Council and trade union branch as well as being an active member of the Labour Party and he gave free advice to the local community. In 1943 Walter took up the post of rehousing and rest centre officer for those who had been blitzed.

Walter understood the value of working class memorabilia and history and in the 1960s he teamed up with Henry Fry and the Trade Union, Labour, Co-operative History Society whose aim was to set-up a Labour History Museum to preserve the people's history and to propagate socialism. Walter donated his unique archive to this cause and his dream was realised when in 1975 the Labour History Museum in Limehouse, London was opened by the then Prime Minister Harold Wilson. Walter saw the museum grow from one room in the old Limehouse Town Hall to the entire building.

Walter had a wicked sense of humour. This was demonstrated when Walter was awarded the Golden Badge of Merit for services to the Labour Party by the then Prime Minister James Callahan: Walter enquired if the warrant was still out for him!.

For his full story, read 'That's the Way it was, a working class autobiography 1890-1950', edited by Terry Philpot and published by New Clarion Press.

T McCarthy, Walter Southgate Trust.

Printed in the United Kingdom by
Lightning Source UK Ltd., Milton Keynes
139844UK00001B/62/P